# Annals of the Dear Unknown

Raised in Wilkes-Barre, Pennsylvania, poet Catherine Chandler spelunks into, excavates, and recovers her Euro-American-settler genealogy, while examining the U.S. Revolutionary War and its disruptions of agricultural endeavour and frontier households, noting the economics of trade with Indigenous peoples and their sometimes violent disaffection with the offerings of settler-interlopers.

In *Annals of the Dear Unknown,* Chandler recognizes that "Uncertainty and ambiguity / must either be rejected or embraced, / leaving room for mystery and truths / more beautiful for having been imagined."

The Richard Wilbur Award-winning bard presents her narrative verse in basically decasyllabic lines in trios of ten-line stanzas. Americans will hear Wilbur, here, but also Longfellow *(Evangeline),* while Canadian readers may be reminded of E.J. Pratt *(Brébeuf and His Brethren).* Whatever the echoes that one may recognize, this verse saga is original, rich with true incident, and even a kind of chronological preface to William Carlos Williams' *Paterson.*

Enjoy here and now these *Annals of the Dear Unknown.*

—George Elliott Clarke, 7th Parliamentary Poet Laureate of Canada
Author, *Where Beauty Survived: An Africadian Memoir* (Knopf, 2021)

# Annals of the Dear Unknown

## A verse-tale

Poems by

Catherine Chandler

Cover design by Shay Culligan
Front cover image, "Dingmans Ferry, PA" by Tommy Kwak.
Photography: tommykwak.com
Instagram: instagram.com/tommykwak


ISBN: 978-1-63980-164-0

Kelsay Books
502 South 1040 East, A-119
American Fork, Utah 84003
Kelsaybooks.com

*In memory of Rachel Tyler Munson*

*(1736–1778)*

# Acknowledgments

Prior to and during the writing of *Annals of the Dear Unknown,* I drew invaluable historical information from hundreds of print and online sources.

However, I wish to especially acknowledge the following persons for their generous assistance: Mark and Amanda at The Luzerne County Historical Society; Sarah and her colleagues at The Lackawanna Historical Society; The Connecticut Historical Society Museum and Library; Aaron McWilliams, Pennsylvania State Archives; writer and historian Mark Dziak; Professor L.H. Roper, State University of New York, New Paltz; Mary McTamaney, City Historian, Newburgh; Bonnie Farver, Tom Adams and Linda Sult, for details on post-revolutionary Berwick; Ed Bishop, for additional information about Wilmot Munson; Laura Redish, for assistance with Lenape orthography and pronunciation; and Tom Munson, historian of the Obadiah Clan of the Munson family, to which the author belongs.

I would also like to express my gratitude to Dr. Paul Riggs, Dean, College of Arts, Humanities and Social Sciences, Wilkes University, for permission to include a poignant line from *A Connecticut Yankee in Penn's Woods: the Life and Times of Thomas Bennet* by Charles E. Myers; and William Thompson, Editor, *Alabama Literary Review,* for publishing the chapters "Together They Come" and "In a Lonely Field."

Finally, a heartfelt thank-you to poets David Mason, Natalie Diaz and Gabrielle Calvocoressi, who have kindly allowed me to use selected lines from their writings as epigraphs in this book. Those by Gabriela Mistral and Robert Frost are in the public domain.

# Author's Note

*Rose's people came from Connecticut.*

That vague description of my great-grandmother, Rose Munson Chandler, as well as a sepia-toned family portrait of Rose sitting alongside her husband, Benjamin Chandler and their three sons, were all I knew as a child of my Munson family history. Like the protagonist in Thomas Campbell's poem, *Gertrude of Wyoming,* I often thought about my "dear unknown" ancestors who had emigrated from Europe to Connecticut, and from there to Pennsylvania.

It wasn't until the death of my father several years ago, when I took possession of an old tome titled *The Munson Record,* that the Munson ancestry came alive for me. In tracing my lineage, generation through generation, back to Captain Thomas Munson who, along with other Pilgrims, sailed to America in 1634, I came across the story of Rose's great-great-grandfather, Obadiah ("Diah") Munson, his wife Rachel Tyler Munson, and their twelve children.

I discovered that I was a descendant of one of those children, Walter Munson, who, with his older brother, Wilmot and other siblings, was part of a frantic departure from the town of Westmoreland at the time of the Battle of Wyoming in Wyoming Valley, Pennsylvania.

During this exodus, known as the Great Runaway, over two thousand frontier settlers were forced to abandon their farms, taking narrow Indian paths and rudimentary roads over mountains and through dense forest areas known as The Great Swamp and The Shades of Death as they made their way to safety hundreds of miles away. Others escaped in canoes and rafts, desperately paddling and poling downstream on the Susquehanna River to Fort Augusta and beyond.

The history of Wyoming Valley, Pennsylvania in the years prior to and during the Yankee-Pennamite Wars and the American Revolution is complex on many levels. It is not the purpose of this book to re-litigate the legal concept and cultural notion concerning the proprietary right of soil. It will not question the wisdom—or lack thereof—of the military decision made on July 3, 1778, nor will it dwell on or dispute conflicting, exaggerated and debunked accounts of the battle's aftermath.

Rather, *Annals of the Dear Unknown* is simply an honest and plainly-told tale, written by someone who, in the words of Ralph Waldo Emerson in his essay *History*, has hoped to "attain and maintain that lofty sight where facts yield their secret sense, and poetry and annals are alike."

—Catherine Chandler

# Contents

Note:

For historical accuracy, the terms Cobb's Mountain, Pennymites, Pittstown, Kingstown, and Wilkesbarre have been retained. These persons and places are now known as Mount Cobb, Pennamites, Pittston, Kingston, and Wilkes-Barre.

# Named Participants (in order of appearance):

*There seems to be a requirement that the play must find its own finale, with participants tossed along impersonally to the end.[1]*

- Little Girl, author of this verse-tale, descendent of Diah Munson and Rachel Tyler Munson
- Nathan Tyler, father of Rachel Tyler Munson
- Obadiah Munson [Sr.] (1703–1773), father of Obadiah ("Diah") Munson
- Rachel Tyler Munson (1736–1778), wife of Diah Munson and mother of their twelve children
- Obadiah ("Diah") Munson (1731–1805), husband of Rachel Tyler Munson
- Barnabas Munson (1754–1792), eldest child of Diah and Rachel
- Uncle Eph, Rachel's uncle Ephraim Tyler
- Granny Doolittle Tuttle, Rachel Tyler Munson's grandmother
- Colonel Eliphalet Dyer, Representative of the Susquehannah Company of Connecticut
- Joel Munson, Diah's uncle
- Wilmot Munson ("Wil") (1755–1845) Diah and Rachel's second child. The protagonist of the story.
- Walter Munson (1771–1836), Diah and Rachel's tenth child
- The twelve Munson children: Barnabas, Wilmot, Hannah, Stephen, Daniel, Ephraim, Irene, Sarah, Obadiah, Walter, Rachel, Benoni (aka John Eton Jones)

---

[1] Myers, Charles E. *A Connecticut Yankee in Penn's Woods: the Life and Times of Thomas Bennet*. Wilkes University Press, 1993, p. 2

- Captain Amos Ogden, Pennsylvanian settler, owner of a fortified blockhouse near Mill Creek
- Francis West "Frank" Phillips, Wyoming Valley settler originally from Rhode Island, Diah's friend
- Private Ichabod Tuttle, Rachel's cousin, killed in the Battle of Wyoming, July 3, 1778
- Elizabeth "Eliza" Matthews Tuttle, Ichabod's wife
- Thankful Tyler Smith, Rachel Tyler Munson's sister
- Doctor William Hooker Smith, physician and minister, Westmoreland
- Lucy Pierce, a girl from Kingstown
- Patience Cooper Munson, Wilmot Munson's wife
- John Phillips, Wilmot Munson's friend, son of Francis Phillips
- Mary Chamberlain Phillips, John's wife
- Meschatamen, Lenape warrior. His Lenape name translates into English as "He who remembers"
- Eton Jones, blacksmith at Fort Brown, one of the Pittstown stockades, friend of Diah Munson
- Rebecca Jones, Eton Jones's wife, wet-nurse to Benoni Munson, mother of Susannah Jones
- Susannah Jones, Rebecca and Eton's daughter
- Ishmael Bennet, another local blacksmith
- Alden Jones, Eton Jones's brother
- Nanny Dunn, local midwife
- Benoni Munson (1778–?), youngest child of Obadiah Munson and Rachel Tyler Munson, adopted by Rebecca Jones and renamed John Eton Jones
- Dr. Lemuel Gustin, local physician
- Dr. Joseph Sprague, one of the first physicians in the Wyoming Valley settlement
- David Inman, Ichabod Tuttle's friend
- Sam Wares, proprietor of a tavern and inn at Shohola

- Eunice Bradley, Diah Munson's second wife
- The Reverend Joshua Williams, pastor, First Church of Christ, Harwinton, Connecticut
- John Eton Jones (1778–unknown), Benoni Munson's adoptive name
- Gerhard Scholl, tailor, Rebecca Jones's second husband

# Proem

*Their lives are part of my life's inventory;*
*my role grows smaller when I glimpse the whole.*
*Today I pocketed a lump of coal.*
*These are the facts, but facts are not the story.*

—David Mason, from *Ludlow*

# Taking Stock

By the middle of the twentieth century,
"King Coal" had been dethroned by natural gas
and oil. In a place tagged Diamond City,
daily life had lost much of its luster.
But to the sad eyes of a little girl
who'd left Poughkeepsie earlier that day,
the glint and glitz of movie house marquees
mirrored in the pitch-black, rain-slicked streets
of Public Square that blustery April night,
Wilkes-Barre spangled, scintillated, shone.

No one had ever told the little girl
that Yankee blood was running through her veins,
nor that the subject of the "Doodle" ditty
had anything at all to do with Rose,
the woman sitting stern and ramrod-straight
in a faded gilt-framed sepia photograph
hanging on an uncle's parlor wall.
It was the present moment, nothing more—
a father far away with polio.
A North End double-block. A soothing thumb.

That night, the little girl slept unaware
that nearly nine score years had come and gone
since Rachel Tyler Munson was interred
along the Susquehanna River's banks,
her children fleeing for their lives; a time
when Eton Jones would chip the glistening rock
from local outcrops for his blacksmith forge,
long before the Knox Mine tragedy.
A time when rival passions for the land
burned like the hot blue flame of anthracite.

# Part One

# Xwewamënk

*How can a century or a heart turn*
*if nobody asks,* Where have all
the natives gone?

—Natalie Diaz, from "Manhattan is a Lenape Word"

# "at the big river flat"


Along the North Branch of the Susquehanna
within the folded Appalachian Mountains
lies a geological depression—
the long, canoe-shaped Ridge and Valley Province.
Before it had a name, when blue-veined ice
receded some twelve thousand years ago,
nomadic hunter-gatherers arrived.
Yet all that one can ever know of them
is what can be divined from potsherds, bones,
tools and weapons carved from stone and wood.


In time, through woodlands dense with oak and birch,
hemlock, hawthorn, hickory, pine and beech,
new men pursued the white-tailed deer and elk.
In spring, with cradleboards upon their backs,
their women broke the soil with deer-bone hoes,
planting seeds of maize and squash and beans.
The Lenape had described this blessed land—
dreamt up by Kishelamakank and formed
by spirits, where a shad-filled river flowed
and waterfowl were plentiful—*Xwewamënk.*

*Wyoming* to the settlers from the east
who claimed the Endless Mountains and the fields,
the forests and the sacred hunting grounds,
attempting to possess what can't be owned,
waging war with brothers over deeds
and documents, until a greater cause
united them in an uneasy peace;
while farther north, Haudenosaunee chiefs,
no longer of one mind, would one day rue
their forfeiture of solidarity.

# The Disposing of Their Children

In January, seventeen forty-six,
Nathan Tyler deeded to his neighbor,
Obadiah Munson, one hundred acres
in Wallingford, Connecticut. The pact
included Tyler's house and barn, its mills,
and the tacit understanding Tyler's daughter
Rachel, nine years old, would wed the younger
Obadiah ("Diah"), then fifteen,
when Rachel came of age. The two men closed
the deal with several tankards of hard cider.


And after seven years had passed, they wed.
When Barnabas, their first of twelve, was born,
Obadiah Senior, out of "love,
good will and natural affection," gave
his son the house and sixty acres of
the selfsame bartered tract. And so began
the young man's unremitting appetite
for land, an uneventful run of years
when gains outnumbered losses. Wallingford
was good. But Diah Munson needed more.

The years went by. They moved to Farmington
where Rachel loved her simple, sturdy home,
her busy life, the brand-new Meeting House,
the blessings and the bounties of the farm,
but felt uneasy when she heard the men
and Wil, their teenaged son, discussing plans
to settle in that godforsaken place
where uncle Ephraim Tyler had outrun
Lenape warriors in '63.
And all the trouble brewing ever since.

# What Reason Weaves

Diah was a superstitious man
who looked for signs and omens in his dreams,
the moon and shooting stars. He'd not abide
a black cat in the barn. He counted crows
and slept feet facing south. Contingent on
the farmland's need—or not—of sun and rain,
he'd find and kill a snake and either hang
or drown it. Even as a little boy
he'd kept a lucky charm—a codfish bone—
and drew his stockings on first left, then right.


His journeys rarely started on a Friday;
he never trimmed his fingernails on Sunday;
and in accordance with the local lore,
he married on a Wednesday afternoon.
Thus Diah was alarmed when Rachel placed
the linsey-woolsey paneled coverlet
that had been passed on down from Granny Tuttle
and Rachel's mother—both of whom had died
not long past forty—on their wedding bed.
He voiced his dread in no uncertain terms.

So Rachel put the coverlet away,
wrapped in calico, where it would lie
unseen, unused, but not unvisited.
For in those rare and scattered unfilled hours,
she'd open up the cedar dowry chest,
remove the coverlet, and lose herself
in the embrace of its remembered scents
and in the white and sky-blue warp and weft
of other lives now absent from her own.
One day it would become a winding sheet.

# A Certain Tract of Land

A piece of paradise. Glib promises
of fertile plains and valleys so unlike
the rocky fields they farmed. Connecticut
was filled with eager, able-bodied men
whose fathers' lands, bequeathed, could not suffice
once divvied up among their many sons.
And so, when Colonel Dyer pitched his scheme
one summer evening at the Meeting House,
two hundred fifty men subscribed at once,
and soon thereafter, some five hundred more.


*How can we possibly go wrong?* they thought,
plunking down five dollars for the chance
to start anew along the Susquehanna.
Although it lay three hundred miles away,
and there were rumors that the land belonged
to Pennsylvania or the Iroquois,
they cast their lot with Dyer and his friends.
Joel Munson, skeptical, declined,
but passed along the word to nephew Diah,
who bought and held a half-share, biding time.

Following the birth of their tenth child,
when he'd disposed of almost everything
he owned in Farmington, one autumn morning
Diah packed a hatchet and an axe,
an adze, a saw, an auger and a mallet,
his firelock, a tinderbox, some shot,
a butcher knife, a skillet and a spoon,
some cornmeal, bread and bacon, applejack,
a woolen blanket, and his deed of sale.
Rachel watched him from the dooryard, silent.

# Part Two

# Wyoming

*O it will be beautiful.*

—Gabrielle Calvocoressi, from "At Last the New Arriving"

# The Anchor

Wilmot Munson, sixteen years of age,
was short and stocky like his father, Diah.
Marked by the gap-toothed smile and dimpled chin
passed on from time to time to Munson sons,
Wil shared Diah's energy and strength,
his keen blue eyes, his fiery red hair,
and most of all his eagerness to move
beyond the boundaries of Connecticut.
But unlike Diah, Wilmot's voice and heart
were softer than his father's ever were.


Born on a summer night when the moon was full,
this second child and second son was quick
to learn the skills reserved for boys and men.
But Rachel, in her wisdom, taught her Wil
not only how to cipher, read and write,
but also all the chief domestic arts—
cooking, sewing, gardening, how to cure
the common illnesses—and by example,
how to live an honorable life
of industry, humility and grace.

Barnabas, the eldest, was away
at Yale when Diah left the family
to clear his pitch in the Wyoming Valley.
Thus it was that Wil, as next in line,
was tasked to stay behind to care for Rachel
and his siblings. He assumed this role
with constancy, but not without a twinge
of wounded pride and smoldering resentment
he tried without success to hide from Rachel,
who knew his thoughts as though they were her own.

# A Darting Fear

Unlike her husband, Diah, who was short,
broad-shouldered, stout, and strong enough to hoist
a barrelful of cider over the rave
of any cart; whose thunderous voice bespoke
the confidence of a successful farmer,
Rachel's strength lay in her fortitude.
Angular, with waist-length auburn hair
and deep-set hazel eyes, this quiet woman
admirably kept house, but kept her peace
where Munson business matters were concerned.


Reserved but cheerful, Rachel baked the bread,
churned the butter, spun the flax and wool,
and filled the featherbeds. She cooked and cleaned,
preserved the pickled beets and damson plums,
made soap and tallow candles, all the while
caring for her children, who were born
like clockwork every second year or so.
That is, till little Walter came along
feet-first. The midwife almost lost them both,
and warned against another pregnancy.

At sundown on the chill October day
when Diah Munson left his family,
before she said her prayers and went to bed,
Rachel, with her homemade bristle brush,
wrested from one hundred gentle strokes
one hundred images of harbored fears.
The whole town knew what Dyer's scouting team
and Uncle Eph had met with years ago
in frontier forests, where not only wolves
and panthers stalked their unsuspecting prey.

# The Signal Tree

Diah Munson, forty years of age,
believed this was his chance—perhaps his last—
to grow his wealth, just as his father had,
with land. And though it lay three hundred miles
away, through virgin woods and wilderness
so thick with undergrowth as to obscure
at times the narrow path he had to take,
he set out on a bright October morning
in seventeen seventy-one, with heady dreams
of farmland on the Susquehanna's banks.


Once Diah left Connecticut and crossed
the Hudson and the Delaware, he took
the Minisink, a path the ancient tribes
had trod for centuries. He made his bed
of hemlock boughs, and slept beneath the stars
or canopies of fragrant conifers,
lighting fires to keep the beasts at bay.
Along the trail, a dome-shaped birch bark hut,
long since abandoned by Lenape hunters,
provided shelter on the night it rained.

The Minisink, once it had passed Shohola,
had risen by degrees to such a height
that, after he had ridden fifteen days,
Diah reached the summit of Cobb's Mountain,
its ridge-top heath so barren that it gave
an unobstructed view of wave on wave
of woodland tree-tops robed in autumn's hues;
and towering above, the signal tree—
a lofty lopstick pine resplendent in
the final rays of the descending sun.

# Promis'd Joy

Other settlers shared in Diah's joy
that day upon the summit of Cobb's Mountain.
They, too, had left their families behind—
for now; but, confident hostilities
with angry Pennymites had been resolved
with Captain Ogden's ousting, they believed
their future in the valley would be bright,
and that, come spring, the town would boast a school,
a Meeting House, impenetrable forts,
a grist mill, and a saw mill, and a name.


The emigrants divided into crews.
Diah, ox-strong, joined the logging team;
likewise Frank Phillips from Rhode Island. Soon
the two became fast friends, and Frank, who claimed
as yet no settling right, helped Diah clear
his lot and daub his hewn-log house. At night,
the tired men bunked down in the Pittstown fort
they called Fort Brown, exchanging tales of home,
though talk of their ambitious dreams eclipsed
all wistfulness for wives and honey cake.

As autumn turned to winter, Diah left,
but Frank stayed on. He manned the Munson right
against intruders, thieves and bogus claims.
In mid-December, Frank obtained the right
to settle in the valley, purchased land,
and built his house along the Lackawanna,
a few miles north of Diah's. Unbeknownst
to these devoted men, their elder sons
would lead—when happiness reversed to sorrow—
their families from a valley set ablaze.

# Corn Planting Moon

The Munson wagon was all set to go—
three yoke of oxen and a dairy cow,
feed, a water barrel and provisions
to last the journey and the summer months,
seeds of corn and wheat and flax, a hoe,
a shovel, scythe and rake, a spinning wheel,
a bucket, pots and pans, their clothes and linens
wrapped in Rachel's heirloom coverlet.
They left the first of May in '72.
A Friday. Diah knew, but let it pass.


Diah walked ahead with the nameless sumpter.
Rachel, Wil, and Stephen manned the wagon.
Daniel, Hannah, Ephraim and Irene
gently spurred the oxen with their goads.
Sarah, Obie and the baby, Walter,
wedged between the boxes and the bales.
The trip was uneventful till they ferried
across the Hudson River at Newburgh Bay,
when, fearing they would surely drown, the children
clung to each other, wailing in dismay.

They met up with the Tuttles one day later—
Rachel's cousin Ichabod and his wife,
Eliza, five months pregnant with their first.
The Minisink, although not much improved
and barely wide enough for them to pass,
was even, high and dry, and more direct
than other paths that led through swamps and bogs.
The last night, when they camped out on Cobb's Mountain,
the Munsons and the Tuttles slept beneath
the full Corn Planting Moon in perigee.

# A Bantam Little Shadow

Diah had planted more than corn that spring.
Rachel, in a late November letter
to her sister, Thankful, back in Wallingford,
described her new life in Wyoming Valley—
the ample, well-built house and open hearth,
the Susquehanna River close at hand,
the flora and the fauna of the forest,
the children diligent and dutiful,
the first year's meager yield of winter wheat.
Her dread at being pregnant once again.


But since she knew no eastbound travelers
to whom she could entrust her forthright letter,
and later, thinking it had seemed too boastful,
while at the same time fearing she might hurt
her sister who had given birth but once,
Rachel burned the letter, page by page,
one night while stirring the next day's cornmeal pottage.
And as she stirred, she thought about the baby
due in three months' time, whose birth, despite
her inner reservations, pleased her husband.

Diah called to mind the midwife's warning
back in Connecticut, and knew the toll
that Walter's birth had taken on his wife,
and yet he welcomed this eleventh child.
Humming to himself Saint David's Tune,
he carved a rocking cradle out of oak
and pledged that, should the baby be a girl,
she'd take her mother's name. And so it was,
that on the twenty-eighth of February,
baby Rachel came into the world.

# Of the Fresh Earth

It started with a mild sore throat that spring,
along with unaccustomed lethargy,
a lingering cough, a hoarseness to his tone
which he attributed to having worked
the previous winter months surveying roads
from Pittstown to the Delaware. All men
who owned a settling right were called upon
to help, from time to time, with its construction.
The daily wage, one shilling sixpence, proved
welcome income in a spartan season.


But Diah had unwittingly brought back
a killer with his pay: diphtheria,
known in that distant age by many names—
throat distemper, children's plague, cynanche.
A week's rest, eel broth, canker root and honey
were all that Diah needed to recover.
But baby Rachel slowly choked, and all
that Doctor William Hooker Smith could do,
both as physician and as man of God,
was offer prayers for her immortal soul.

Little Walter did not understand
the reason why his siblings sobbed and bawled;
and in the doleful days and weeks that followed,
Wilmot took them all under his wing,
watching his parents mourn, each in their way.
Rachel went about her daily tasks,
grateful that the others had been spared.
Diah laid his daughter in the earth,
pursed his lips, took up his axe, and chopped
the little cradle into firewood.

# Fair Laughs the Morn

The settlement now had a name: Westmoreland.
Connecticut had legally attached
the town to Litchfield, many miles away.
The residents felt safe and more secure,
and with a confidence—however flawed—
fell to the business of enacting rules
and regulations, building schools and mills,
improving roads, providing for defense,
expelling bogus Yankees, working hard,
but worshiping and resting on the Sabbath.


Wilmot Munson, twenty-one, had bought
a half-right in the upper Pittstown district
near the confluence of the Lackawanna
and the Susquehanna, where, in time,
he hoped to build a home and raise a family.
Since spring, he had been courting Lucy Pierce,
a tall, outspoken, buxom honey-blonde
from Kingstown, who invariably won
the river common spinning bees, and wore
her homespun frocks with patriotic pride.

This interval of peace would not last long—
the Continental Army needed men.
Three Munson sons were quick to heed the call
in June of '75, though Wil returned
the following March when Boston was secured.
But in the meantime, faithless Lucy Pierce
had switched her loyalties and bundled with
a Tory, had a child, and moved away.
Wil harbored no resentment toward the girl.
Years later, he would marry Patience Cooper.

## "He who remembers"

As Diah Munson and two hundred more—
and then two thousand more—arrived to settle
with their families in Wyoming Valley,
most Lenape had already left
for Wyalusing and Ohio, though
from time to time they made their way downriver,
exchanging bear and beaver pelts for tools,
textiles, blankets, guns and alcohol,
weighing Yankee-Pennymite enmity,
eventually siding with the latter.


One Sunday afternoon in '77,
John Phillips—son of Frank—his wife and children,
while foraging in the fields and open woodlands
for morels, wild strawberries and chicory,
met up with hunters of the Munsee tribe
who'd likely traveled downstream from Tioga
to barter at the Wilkesbarre trading post.
Mary pulled the children close, while John,
who sensed no danger, cautiously approached
the obvious leader of the group, and smiled.

Meschatamen—a tall, tattooed young man
with penetrating eyes, who knew enough
of English to get by—held out a haunch
of venison, a turkey and a buckskin,
in exchange for Scout, the quarter horse,
John's linen shirt and Mary's cap and bonnet.
John hoped the trade, though disproportionate,
perhaps had gained their trust and amity.
Meschatamen and John would meet again
one summer night, within a year or so.

# Part Three

# Westmoreland

*If they could, the trees would lift you*
*and carry you from valley to valley,*
*and you would pass from arm to arm,*
*as a child walks from father to father.*

—Gabriela Mistral, from "Bosque del pino"
(translation by Catherine Chandler)

# The Finer Forge

Eton Jones's simple blacksmith forge
was situated in the Pittstown fort
where Diah Munson owned Lot Number 5.
The shop was dark and reeked of molten iron,
coal dust, quenching metal, copious sweat.
Though mainly sought out as a farrier,
Eton Jones, a Patriot at heart,
in bold defiance of the British law,
produced the township settlers' scythes and spades,
their axes, wheel rims, cowbells, pots and pans.


Jones was a buoyant, easygoing man
whose raucous singing often could be heard
above the cadenced clanging of the hammer
and the relentless breathing of the bellows.
He never pressed a customer for pay,
and often bartered horseshoes for a sack
of cornmeal, chestnuts or a beaver tail.
This vexed his solid, levelheaded wife,
Rebecca, who equated industry
with reckonings in shillings, pence and pounds.

And there was money to be made each spring—
shad season on the Susquehanna River,
a time when Eton Jones and Diah Munson
would drag a seine in tandem on its banks.
In May of '78, when they had netted
thirty barrels of the spawning fish,
their cheerfulness at such a bounteous catch
was overshadowed by disturbing news
of raids and disappearances upriver
and sightings of the Tories at Tioga.

# The Mystic Shining Cup

One fine June morning, after the spawning run
was over, Eton Jones, as was his custom
when running low on stone coal for his forge,
took up his pickax, shovel, several sacks,
and rode his packhorse up near Dial Rock
to dig as many lumps of shiny black
slow-burning anthracite as he might need
to get him through the month. His wife, Rebecca,
had given birth to their first child, a girl
they named Susannah, just the day before.

As he approached the outcrop site, the warmth
of the noonday sun upon his back, the scent
of laurel blossoms, and the lively chorus
of nesting thrush and warblers filled the man
with such a sense of cheer and raw contentment
that his wild rendition of the Liberty Song
rang through the air and echoed off the hills.
He made a mental note to gather up
an armload of the laurel for his wife
on his return trip to the settlement.

Afterwards, as Eton Jones was loading
the sacks of coal and tools into his cart,
three Seneca appeared, unhitched the horse,
shot Eton through the heart, and took his scalp.
Later in the day, another blacksmith,
Ishmael Bennet, came upon the scene
and brought the body back to the stockade.
Eton's brother, Alden, buried him
and urged Rebecca, numb with grief and fear,
to gear up for a move to Fort Augusta.

# A Joyless Eye

Bound Brook. Brandywine. Germantown.
Valley Forge. As Stephen Munson spoke
of all he'd seen and done the past three years
while serving in the Continental Army,
his parents listened in intense alarm.
Knowing that the war was far from over
despite the victory at Saratoga,
and that the current military stalemate
meant the outcome could go either way,
Stephen kept his musket at the ready.


A sweltering heat wave swept across the valley.
As danger lurked upon the edges of
Westmoreland, Rachel, with a baby due
in late July, endured a weightiness,
not only from the pregnancy and heat,
but even more so from her husband's absence.
Believing he had ample time to ride
to Farmington and back, to find a place
where they could all ride out the war in peace,
Diah had left them in the care of Wil.

Wil hid provisions in a hollow log
and left the family livestock free to roam.
He buried stores beneath the floor. He lent
Rebecca Jones his fifteen-foot canoe.
But there was nothing he could do about
the newly-planted sweet corn or the flax
and barley harvests of the coming weeks.
Then, one stifling late-June afternoon,
just as a new moon veiled the blistering sun,
Rachel fetched the birth-stool from the barn.

# Son of My Sorrow

Eliza Tuttle and Rebecca Jones
arrived, children in tow, at Diah's house,
prepared for any length of lying-in.
They tried their best to soften Rachel's dread
at this one's coming well before its time,
legs kicking low, its head beneath her ribs.
But Scripture only added to her fears.
The local midwife, Nanny Dunn, smeared grease,
bound the nascent baby's feet with cloth,
and eased him out into a world of hurt.


Why Rachel named her newborn son Benoni
can only be conjectured. She had borne
her labor pains as well as in the past.
Though undersized, his cries were deafening.
With plentiful red hair and dimpled chin,
he was the image of his father. Still,
her brow was furrowed with anxiety,
a pins-and-needles sense of worriment.
Perhaps it was the solar eclipse, or
the flame-like port-wine stain upon his cheek.

Rebecca and Eliza cooked and cleaned
and tended to the children. Two days later,
when Rachel asked her eldest daughter, Hannah,
to fetch the heirloom coverlet—for she
felt cold despite the heat—then threw it off,
her breathing short and quick, her milk suppressed,
Stephen went to bring back Dr. Smith
or Dr. Gustin. Neither one arrived,
both being in mourning for their wives, who'd died
of childbed fever just the week before.

Ben-Oni, translated from the Hebrew language, means "son of my sorrow."

# Her Cabin'd, Ample Spirit

Stephen found and brought back Doctor Sprague,
who breathed his patient's vein, to no avail.
Rachel Tyler Munson, forty-two,
had reached the limits of her breeding life.
As June progressed into July, she passed.
The turmoil in the Munson house was such
that Wil and Stephen barely could control
the desperate keening of the younger ones.
Rebecca volunteered to nurse Benoni,
to which expedient Wil acquiesced.


Besides the doctor, Stephen Munson brought
frightful news of an immense flotilla
of Tories, Loyalists and Iroquois
descending the Susquehanna towards Westmoreland.
Families were flocking to the forts,
and Wil knew they would need to leave before
a proper funeral could be arranged.
His Fort Brown friends helped Wil dig Rachel's grave
in the burial ground along the riverbank,
and built for her a rough-hewn pine box coffin.

They used the white and sky-blue coverlet
for Rachel Tyler Munson's shroud, but some
was cut away for a blanket for Benoni.
Wil and Stephen set a sandstone rock
to mark the burial site until such time
as they'd return with Diah to retrieve
their baby brother from Rebecca Jones;
when they would place a proper death's-head  marker
for the one whose pious psalm-tune lullabies
would sing forever in their broken hearts.

# The Burning Sky

Wil could see and smell the colonnades
of acrid smoke rising from Fort Jenkins
across the river from the Munson farm.
His packhorse, loaded for the journey back
to Farmington, stood stock-still in the heat.
He quickly gathered up his frightened siblings,
gave Rebecca Jones a haversack
of money for Benoni, and departed,
taking—as Diah had—the east-west road,
assuming they would meet up on the trail.


Rebecca Jones was ready. When she heard
the drumbeats and the fifer's piercing notes
of On Saint Patrick's Day, and soon thereafter,
musket-fire and whoops, she grabbed Wil's cash,
the proceeds from the shad sales, the saltpeter
ten-pound bounty she had earned, and laid
Susannah and Benoni in the boat,
hopped in, and paddled down toward Fort Augusta,
drifting when the babies wailed for milk
or when she took a snack of bread and rum.

Stephen Munson stayed behind. He'd taken
the ferry to Forty Fort and volunteered.
Though wounded in the foot, he made his way
across the meadows and the fields, until
he reached the riverbank. Then, after dark,
he slowly swam back to the eastern shore,
unhitched the horse he'd hidden the woods
and rode away, the air pervaded by
the stench of burning flesh and by the howls
of Patriots he was helpless to set free.

# Departed

Eliza Tuttle waited anxiously
at Forty Fort throughout that hideous night.
As one by one the women learned the fates
of fathers, sons and husbands, any hope
she held out for her Ichabod's return
was dashed when David Inman told of how
his friend had been pursued by Seneca,
then shot and scalped before he reached the river.
Her husband dead, her home burnt to the ground,
Eliza and her sons fled to the mountains.


John Phillips and his family left their farm
for Fort Brown and the Blanchard garrison.
The settlers' livestock had been freed or stolen,
crops destroyed, cabins sacked and torched.
One night, Lenape warriors appeared,
commanding all the refugees to leave.
Meschatamen recognized the man
who'd given him his shirt and quarter horse.
He painted John and Mary's foreheads black,
thus promising safe passage through the woods.

Wilkesbarre lay in ruins. Those who could,
hastily built rafts and poled downstream
to Fort Augusta and beyond. But most
trekked through the Poconos. Some wandered off
and were not seen again. Though many died
of sickness, sheer exhaustion and despair,
Eliza Tuttle, her sons, the Phillipses,
and hundreds more at last attained the fort
at Stroudsburg, with accounts of devastation
almost too harrowing to be believed.

# Together They Come

As Wilmot shepherded the family
across the Minisink's first sixty miles,
he anguished over what had come to pass—
his mother dead, Benoni given up,
the settlement about to be destroyed,
the grief soon to befall his father, Diah.
He knew the dangers lurking in the woods,
yet sensed a deep and unseen power of grace.
Little Walter walked most of the way
and rarely asked to ride the patient horse.


As Diah rode back from Connecticut,
unsettling news he'd heard along the way
from families heading eastward on the trail
made sleep next to impossible. He reached
the shallow crossing on the Delaware
and stopped to rest his horse and stay the night
at Sam Wares' inn and tavern at the clearing
Lenape named Shohola—Place of Peace.
He rose at daybreak, hoping to be back
with Rachel well before the week was out.

Diah saw them first. Bedraggled, barefoot,
at the water's edge, waiting their turn
to mount the horse and ford the Delaware.
Beside himself with joy, he cried out, *Wil!*
then realized that Rachel wasn't there.
On hearing every detail of his loss,
Diah neither wept nor censured God;
but, shouldering the blame for everything
that had occurred, he barely spoke a word
as they made their way back to Connecticut.

# In a Lonely Field

For weeks marauders made their presence known
in what was once Westmoreland. As they left
the scene of carnage, so did all the circling,
hissing, satiated turkey vultures,
who, for now at least, would have to settle
for an injured warbler or a woodland vole.
In late October, settlers who'd returned
to salvage what they could of wasting crops
were ordered to recover and inter
the remains of those who'd perished in July.


Distinctive shoes helped to identify
a few of them, but not with certainty,
for most had been reduced to scattered bones
and rotting rags. The men dug two mass graves
and laid their families and friends to rest
as best they could. The Battle of Wyoming
lived on in the collective memory,
though older settlers died and new ones came
to harvest trees and later mine for coal.
A monument would mark the sacred site.

Diah Munson never did go back
to place a proper headstone on the grave
of Rachel Tyler Munson, wife and mother
of their dozen children, living, dead, and lost.
Within six months he married Eunice Bradley,
a cousin whom he kept as bedmate, cook
and nanny. And because the Pennymites
had occupied his Susquehanna claim—
and later were awarded title to it—
Diah bought a grist mill and moved on.

# Part Four

## Pennsylvania and Beyond

*The woods are lovely, dark and deep,*
*But I have promises to keep . . .*

—Robert Frost, from "Stopping by Woods on a Snowy Evening"

# His Place in the Family of Things

More than a quarter century would pass
before the Reverend Joshua Williams preached
at Diah Munson's funeral. Meanwhile,
his fifth son, Ephraim, enlisted and
survived the war. But Daniel, who had served
as Life Guard under General Nathanael Green,
died of typhus following the siege
of Yorktown. Every effort Diah made
to find Benoni ended in defeat.
Wil promised he would keep the search alive.


It was impossible for him to know
that, as the years went by, the names had changed.
Having had no news from Diah Munson,
Rebecca moved to Harris' Ferry, where
she raised Benoni as John Eton Jones,
"twin brother" to Susannah. Afterward,
Rebecca married tailor Gerhard Scholl;
so anyone attempting to locate
the widow Jones and young Benoni Munson
would only meet with bitter disappointment.

Time, as it must, went on. As businessman
as well as farmer, Diah recommenced
his dealings in immoveable property
in Northbury and later, Harwinton.
Though often he'd bemoan each wasted cent
he'd sunk into the grim "Wyoming disaster,"
Diah never spoke about the loss
of Rachel, baby Rachel, or Benoni.
Their souls inhabited his quiet hours,
their absence weighing on his failing heart.

# Wil's Word

Wilmot Munson loved Wyoming Valley.
But one more war with Pennymites, two floods,
and twenty years of drawn-out legal wrangling
went by before the courts would recognize
the early settlers' private right of soil
and compensate for losses they'd sustained.
Westmoreland, once a town, was history.
And as the eighteenth century neared its end,
Wilmot bought a farm and apple orchard
near Toby Creek in Trucksville, Luzerne County.


Wil learned, to his dismay, about the flood
of '84, and how the Susquehanna,
swollen by unseasonable rain
and choked with massive floes of melting ice,
had swept away all houses, livestock, fences,
hay and grain, and even burial grounds—
including Rachel's—lying along its banks.
He felt as if he'd let his mother down;
yet one more promise he had made to Diah
and to himself remained to keep: Benoni.

He spent the winters visiting the farms
of all the elder settlers in the townships
for clues, however insignificant,
but came up empty-handed. Everyone
for miles around knew Wil was on a quest—
a wild-goose chase, to some. The word got out.
It traveled over roads and forest trails;
it rode on merchants' arks and timber rafts
downstream and back again. But it was Wil
who found Benoni, quite by accident.

# Unable To Close the Distance

The Munson farm and orchard had combined
a local market trade—the bartering
of family surplus crops for metal goods,
molasses, liquor, salt and cloth—with one
where ample yields of produce, wheat and rye
found marketplaces far afield. The year
Wil drove a loaded cart of apples down
to Berwick, twenty miles away, his wife
had asked him to bring back some sewing needles,
buttons, and a hat for Wilmot Jr.


Jones Mercantile & Millinery stood
at Market Street and Second. Jones's wife
—Wil had surmised—was measuring a length
of cotton for a customer. Wil browsed
the store for hats, and hoped perhaps, despite
the prevalence of Joneses . . . Someone asked
if he might be of help. As Wilmot turned
and faced the likeness of his younger self,
he knew his search was at an end. *Benoni!*
The terse reply, *The name's John Eton Jones.*

John listened skeptically as Wil recounted
the sad events that ushered in this moment.
Rachel's death. The willing wet-nurse friend.
The exodus in opposite directions.
His dying father's quest to find the child.
John disavowed all knowledge of the Munsons,
but granted that he had a twin, Susannah,
that his late mother's name had been Rebecca,
but brusquely brushed it off as happenstance.
The birthmark on his cheek told otherwise.

# All Ye Need to Know

[*The Susquehanna Democrat,* Wilkesbarre, Pennsylvania,
8 October, 1819. List of unclaimed letters
at the Post Office, one addressed to Walter Munson.]

John Eton Jones—himself a foster-child
of silence and slow time—as time went on,
surmounted incredulity and all
the turmoil and resentment he had felt
at realizing he'd been lost, then found.
He learned that Wil had sold the Trucksville farm
to Walter Munson, so he wrote to ask
his brother for Wil's forwarding address.
Walter claimed the letter, sent it on
to Wil who, overcome with joy, replied.

[*The Democratic Pioneer*, Upper Sandusky, Ohio,
February 2, 1849. List of unclaimed letters
at the Post Office, one addressed to Wilmot Munson.]

As time went on, John Eton Jones and Wil,
though never having met again, kept up
infrequent correspondence. Wil had left
Chenango for Ohio when his wife,
Patience Cooper Munson, passed away.
John Eton Jones, now seventy years old,
in an instinctive moment of nostalgia,
had signed this latest letter as Benoni;
but Wil had died in eighteen-forty-five.
The unclaimed letter was at length returned.

There's only so much one can know for sure
in an attempt to trace the dear unknown.
Uncertainty and ambiguity
must either be rejected or embraced,
leaving room for mystery and truths
more beautiful for having been imagined.
Those unclaimed letters did, in fact, exist.
But were they written by John Eton Jones?
And was it true the last one held a swatch
of white and sky-blue linsey-woolsey cloth?

# Position of the Wyoming Forts, 1770s

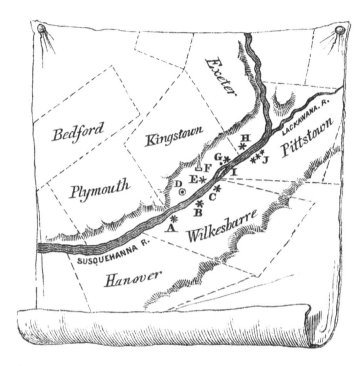

Description:

A Marks the site of Fort Durkee; B, Wyoming or Wilkesbarre Fort;
C, Fort Ogden; D, Village of Kingston; E, Forty Fort;
F, the battleground; G, Wintermoot's Fort; H, Fort Jenkins;
I, Monocasy Island; J, the three Pittstown stockades

Source: Benson J. Lossing, *Pictorial Field-Book of the Revolution,* vol. 1, p. 353. Harper and Brothers, 1851

Map Credit: Courtesy of the private collection of Roy Winkelman, PhD, Projects and Permissions Manager, Florida Center for Instructional Technology, College of Education, University of South Florida

# Map of the Minisink and Other Paths

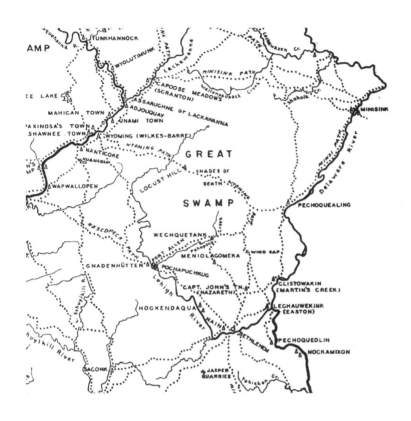

Pennsylvania State Archives/MG-192

Source: Wallace, Paul A.W. *Indian Paths of Pennsylvania.*
Pennsylvania Historical and Museum Commission, Pennsylvania
State Archives, 1965

# Selected Bibliography

Boyd, Julian P., and Robert J. Taylor. *The Susquehannah Company Papers*. Wyoming Historical & Geological Society, 1930.

Bushman, Richard Lyman. "Markets and Composite Farms in Early America." *The William and Mary Quarterly*, vol. 55, no. 3, 1998, pp. 351–374.

Campbell, Thomas. *Gertrude of Wyoming; or, The Pennsylvanian Cottage*. D. Appleton & Co., 1858.

Chapman, Isaac A. *Sketch of the History of Wyoming*. S.D. Lewis, 1830.

DeLacy, Margaret. "Puerperal Fever in Eighteenth-century Britain." *Bulletin of the History of Medicine*, vol. 63, no. 4, 1989, pp. 521–556.

Dunn, Mary Maples. "Saints and Sisters: Congregational and Quaker Women in the Early Colonial Period." *American Quarterly*, vol. 30, no. 5, 1978, pp. 582–601.

Dye, Nancy Schrom. "History of Childbirth in America." *Signs*, vol. 6, no. 1, 1980, pp. 97–108.

Dziak, Mark G. *The Battle of Wyoming: for Liberty and Life: the Whole Story of the 1778 Battle and Massacre in Wyoming Valley, Pennsylvania*. The Author, 2008.

Egle, William Henry, ed. *Documents Relating to the Connecticut Settlement in the Wyoming Valley*. E.K. Meyers, 1890.

Grubb, Farley. "German Immigration to Pennsylvania, 1709 to 1820." *The Journal of Interdisciplinary History*, vol. 20, no. 3, 1990, pp. 417–436.

Harvey, Oscar Jewell. *A History of Wilkes-Barré, Luzerne County, Pennsylvania, from its First Beginnings to the Present Time: Including Chapters of Newly-discovered Early Wyoming Valley History, Together with Many Biographical Sketches and Much Genealogical Material.* Raeder Press, 1927.

*Historical and Biographical Annals of Columbia and Montour Counties.* J.H. Beers & Co., 1915.

Hollister, Horace. *Contributions to the History of the Lackawanna Valley.* W.H. Tinson, 1857.

Johnson, Ella Roberts. *History of Pittston. - taken from a manuscript of notes compiled in the years 1910–1912.* http://greaterpittstonhistory.org/wp-content/uploads/2014/04/EC-Johnson-Pittston-History-Part-1.pdf.

Johnston, Henry P., ed. *The Record of Connecticut Men in the Military and Naval Service During the War of the Revolution 1775–1783.* Case, Lockwood & Brainard, 1889.

Joyce, Mary Hinchcliffe. *Pioneer Days in the Wyoming Valley.* S.n., 1928.

Lossing, Benjamin J. *The Pictorial Field-Book of the Revolution; or, Illustrations, by Pen and Pencil, of the History, Biography, Scenery, Relics, and Traditions of the War for Independence.* Harper & Bros., 1851.

Lottick, Sally Teller. *Wyoming Valley's Earliest Settlers.* Wyoming Historical and Geological Society, 1997.

Lowens, Irving. "The Bay Psalm Book in 17th-Century New England." *Journal of the American Musicological Society*, vol. 8, no. 1, 1955, pp. 22–29.

Lutnick, S. M. "The Harassed History of Bundling." *The School Review*, vol. 70, no. 2, 1962, pp. 233–239.

Main, Gloria L. "Naming Children in Early New England." *The Journal of Interdisciplinary History*, vol. 27, no. 1, 1996, pp. 1–27.

Matthews, Alfred. *History of Wayne, Pike, and Monroe Counties, Pennsylvania.* R.T. Peck & Company, 1886.

Miller-Lanning, Darlene. "Dark Legend and Sad Reality: Peck's Wyoming and Civil War." *Pennsylvania History: A Journal of Mid-Atlantic Studies*, vol. 65, no. 4, 1998, pp. 405–444.

Miner, Charles. *History of Wyoming, in a Series of Letters, from Charles Miner, to His Son, William Penn Miner, Esq.* J. Crissy, 1845.

Munsell, W. W. *History of Luzerne, Lackawanna and Wyoming Counties, Penna.* W.W. Munsell & Co., 1880.

Munson, Myron Andrews. *1637 – 1887 The Munson Record: a Genealogical and Biographical Account of Captain Thomas Munson (A Pioneer of Hartford and New Haven) and His Descendants.* Printed for The Munson Association by The Tuttle, Morehouse & Taylor Press, 1895.

Myers, Charles E. *A Connecticut Yankee in Penn's Woods: the Life and Times of Thomas Bennet.* Wilkes University Press, 1993.

New England Historical and Genealogical Register. *Following Connecticut Ancestors to Pennsylvania: Susquehanna Company Settlers.* The New England Historical and Genealogical Society, 1985.

Ousterhout, Anne M. "Frontier Vengeance: Connecticut Yankees vs. Pennamites in the Wyoming Valley." *Pennsylvania History: A Journal of Mid-Atlantic Studies*, vol. 62, no. 3, 1995, pp. 330–363.

Pearce, Stewart. *Annals of Luzerne County: a Record of Interesting Events, Traditions and Anecdotes, from the First Settlement in Wyoming Valley to 1866.* J. B. Lippingcott & Co., 1866.

Peck, George. *Wyoming; Its History, Stirring Incidents, and Romantic Adventures.* Harper & Bros., 1858.

Scholten, Catherine M. "'On the Importance of the Obstetrick Art': Changing Customs of Childbirth in America, 1760 to 1825." *The William and Mary Quarterly*, vol. 34, no. 3, 1977, pp. 426–445.

Treckel, Paula A. "Breastfeeding and Maternal Sexuality in Colonial America." *The Journal of Interdisciplinary History*, vol. 20, no. 1, 1989, pp. 25–51.

Wallace, Paul A.W. *Indian Paths of Pennsylvania.* Pennsylvania Historical and Museum Commission, 1965.

Westerkamp, Marilyn J. "Engendering Puritan Religious Culture in Old and New England." *Pennsylvania History: A Journal of Mid-Atlantic Studies*, vol. 64, 1997, pp. 105–122.

Weyburn, Samuel Fletcher. *Following the Connecticut Trail from the Delaware River to the Susquehanna Valley.* The Anthracite Press, Inc., 1932.

Wyoming Historical and Geological Society. *Proceedings and Collections of the Wyoming Historical and Geological Society.* E.B. Yordy, 1898.

# About the Author

Catherine Chandler is the author of six poetry collections, including *Lines of Flight,* shortlisted for the Poets' Prize, and *The Frangible Hour,* winner of the Richard Wilbur Award. She was raised in Wilkes-Barre, Pennsylvania.

After graduating from Wilkes University, Chandler emigrated to Canada, completing postgraduate studies at McGill University, Montreal, where, prior to her retirement, she held various administrative and academic appointments, including International Affairs Officer and Course Lecturer, Department of Translation Studies.

Chandler's poems, translations, stories, essays and reviews have been published in print and online journals and anthologies in North America, Europe and Australia. Several of Chandler's poems were chosen by George Elliott Clarke, Poet Laureate of Canada, for inclusion in the National Poetry Registry, Library of Parliament.

Reviews of Chandler's books, audio recordings, and other information are available at her poetry blog, *The Wonderful Boat,* at cathychandler.blogspot.com.

Made in United States
Orlando, FL
30 November 2022

25295715R00061